Prevent Addiction to Smartphones

ANNAMA REDDY CHAMUNDESWARI

(Author, Counselling Psychologist and
Specializing in geriatric counselling)

Prevent Addiction to Smartphones

Author: Annama Reddy Chamundeswari

ISBN: 978 - 93 - 340 -4491 - 1

Category: Psychology / Philosophy

© Annama Reddy Chamundeswari

Edition: 2024

Email :

counsellingpsychologistchamu@gmail.com

CONTENTS

FOREWARD

Smartphone addiction is increasingly recognized as a prevalent issue in modern society, representing a significant manifestation of the ongoing crisis surrounding technology and mental health. The pervasive nature of smartphone addiction has become a concerning phenomenon, with individuals of all ages being affected by its detrimental effects on their well-being. This addiction to smartphones is evident in the compulsive need to constantly check and engage with mobile devices, leading to decreased social interactions, sleep disturbances, and a decline in overall productivity.

The impact of smartphone addiction extends beyond just personal behavior, as it also has broader implications for societal norms and relationships. The incessant use of smartphones can contribute to the erosion of meaningful face-to-face communication, resulting in diminished social skills and a sense of disconnectedness among individuals. This growing reliance on smartphones for entertainment, communication, and information has created a dependency that can be difficult to break, further exacerbating the negative consequences associated with this addiction.

Addressing the root causes of smartphone addiction requires a multifaceted approach that involves raising awareness, promoting digital wellness practices, and encouraging mindful technology use. By fostering a culture of digital balance and mindfulness, individuals can strive to regain control over their smartphone usage and prioritize healthier habits that support their overall well-being. In doing so, we can begin to mitigate the detrimental effects of smartphone addiction and create a more sustainable relationship with technology in our lives.

In today's digital age, saving the future generation from the pitfalls of smart phone addiction has become an increasingly urgent and complex task. With the pervasive use of smartphones among children and teenagers, concerns about detrimental impacts on their physical, mental, and emotional well-being have escalated. As responsible adults, it is our duty to explore effective strategies and implement comprehensive measures to mitigate the risks associated with excessive smartphone usage.

To address this pressing issue, setting clear boundaries and establishing healthy tech habits within families and educational institutions is paramount. Parents and teachers should prioritize open communication, fostering a supportive environment where youngsters can express their concerns and seek guidance without fear of judgment. By promoting a balanced lifestyle that encompasses outdoor activities, creative pursuits, and face-to-face interactions, we can gradually reduce the allure of constant digital engagement.

Equipping young individuals with digital literacy skills and encouraging critical thinking is crucial in empowering them to make informed choices regarding their online behavior. Collaborating with mental health professionals and technology experts can further enhance our understanding of the psychological and neurological implications of smartphone addiction, enabling us to tailor interventions that address underlying root causes and promote sustainable recovery.

Safeguarding the future generation from smart phone addiction demands a holistic approach that combines community awareness, education, and proactive intervention. By working together and leveraging the collective wisdom of diverse stakeholders, we can cultivate a generation that is equipped to navigate the digital landscape responsibly, fostering well-rounded individuals who thrive both online and offline.

###

Smart Phone Addiction

Mobile addiction is a prevalent modern phenomenon that has escalated as smartphones have become widely adopted and integrated into everyday life in recent years. This addiction entails an excessive focus on the mobile device and personalized usage patterns, such as repetitive checking of emails and text messages, often at the expense of other activities. The pervasive nature of mobile addiction is characterized by an incessant urge to engage with the device, leading to a neglect of more productive endeavors and a detrimental impact on various aspects of one's well-being.

The detrimental effects of mobile addiction can manifest in several areas, including mental health, social interactions, academic performance, and occupational productivity. The compulsion to constantly utilize the mobile device can disrupt cognitive processes, diminish social connections, hinder academic learning, and impede professional responsibilities. Furthermore, the sedentary behavior associated with prolonged mobile device use can contribute to physical discomfort and musculoskeletal issues due to prolonged periods of sitting in static positions.

The emergence of mobile addiction as a significant concern underscores the importance of establishing healthy tech habits and fostering a balanced relationship with digital devices. Strategies to address mobile addiction may include setting designated device-free times, implementing digital detox practices, and prioritizing real-world interactions over virtual engagement. By recognizing the potential harms of excessive mobile device usage and proactively managing one's relationship with technology, individuals can mitigate the negative consequences associated with mobile addiction and promote overall well-being.

As society continues to grapple with the evolving impact of technology on daily life, addressing the prevalence of mobile addiction represents a critical step towards cultivating a more mindful and balanced approach to digital consumption. By raising awareness about the risks of unchecked mobile device usage and encouraging responsible device management, individuals can safeguard their mental, social, and physical health while cultivating a healthier and more sustainable relationship with technology in the digital age.

In the past decade, a noticeable trend has emerged wherein an increasing number of individuals have developed addiction-like behaviors towards their mobile devices. This phenomenon is particularly prominent among individuals who exhibit signs of obsession with their phones, resulting in a variety of symptoms that suggest a dependency on these technological devices.

One behavior commonly observed is the tendency to spend excessive amounts of time on one's phone, even when there are no pressing tasks or needs to attend to. This constant engagement often extends to the habitual checking of messages and notifications, seeking updates or new information that might be available. Moreover, the overuse of social media applications such as Facebook and Instagram has become a prevalent issue, contributing to the overall obsession with mobile devices.

Individuals who experience this addiction-like behavior often turn to their devices as a form of escapism, using them to avoid confronting other responsibilities or challenges they might prefer to ignore. This reliance on mobile devices can lead to a perpetual sense of needing to use them, even in inappropriate situations, as individuals find excuses to justify their constant connectivity.

There is a noticeable pattern of individuals wanting privacy while engaged with their phones, indicating a desire to shield their behaviors from others' scrutiny. The inability to go for extended periods without checking messages or updates showcases a deep-rooted dependency on these devices for constant connection and validation.

Individuals experiencing this form of addiction often report feelings of restlessness and irritability when deprived of their phones, underscoring the psychological reliance they have developed. Even when anxious about the flood of notifications lighting up their screens, individuals find themselves compelled to check each one, perpetuating a cycle of dependency reinforced by technology's addictive qualities.

***

Effective Methods to Overcome from Smartphone Addiction

In contemporary society, with mobile phones becoming an indispensable part of everyday life, it is not uncommon for people to struggle with mobile addiction. However, several strategies can be applied to overcome this modern challenge. One effective tip is to maintain distance from your phone throughout the day by physically keeping it out of sight. By implementing this practice, individuals can reduce the habitual urge to constantly check their phones in anticipation of updates. When the phone is not within reach at all times, the temptation to look for notifications diminishes as the immediate reward of checking the device is no longer readily available. This creates a space for individuals to refocus their attention on more meaningful activities, fostering a healthier relationship with technology. Another useful tactic is to power off the phone before bedtime. Engaging in this practice enables individuals to disconnect from digital stimuli and promote better sleep quality. By turning off the phone, individuals eliminate potential disturbances during the night, allowing for a more restful and rejuvenating sleep experience. Through these proactive measures, individuals can gradually reduce their reliance on mobile devices and reclaim control over their tech usage.

The key to effectively combating phone addiction lies in the conscious practice of avoidance. By recognizing the dangers of excessive phone usage and taking proactive measures to limit your interaction with it, you create a foundation for healthier habits. One way to achieve this is by establishing clear boundaries around your phone usage, prioritizing its functionality and utility over mindless scrolling. Deleting superfluous apps that only serve to consume your time and attention can significantly reduce the temptation to indulge in excessive phone use. Instead, consider redirecting your focus toward activities that foster genuine connections with others, such as engaging in face-to-face conversations or participating in group outings. Embracing these alternate modes of communication not only helps curb phone addiction but also enriches your social interactions and overall well-being. Furthermore, cultivating mindfulness around your phone habits enables you to stay present in the moment, allowing you to fully engage with your surroundings without constant digital distractions. In essence, by deliberately choosing when and how to use your phone, you empower yourself to break free from the grips of addiction and lead a more balanced and fulfilling life.

By nurturing an environment of transparent communication, implementing clear boundaries, and actively promoting various other beneficial activities, adults play a pivotal role in guiding young individuals towards cultivating positive relationships with their smartphones. Excessive reliance on cell phones can potentially result in a range of physical and psychological issues. It is crucial for adults to educate themselves on the warning signs of cellphone addiction and to be equipped with effective strategies to aid young individuals in overcoming detrimental habits relating to smartphone usage. A multifaceted approach that involves engaging young individuals in alternative activities such as sports, hobbies, or social interactions can significantly contribute to reducing their dependence on smartphones. Moreover, creating an open dialogue about the implications of excessive phone usage, setting limits on screen time, and encouraging mindfulness and self-awareness are vital components of supporting healthy smartphone habits in young individuals. Ultimately, by fostering a balanced and harmonious relationship with technology, adults can empower the younger generation to embrace a more well-rounded and fulfilling lifestyle that prioritizes mental and physical well-being over excessive screen time.

***

Signs of Phone Addiction

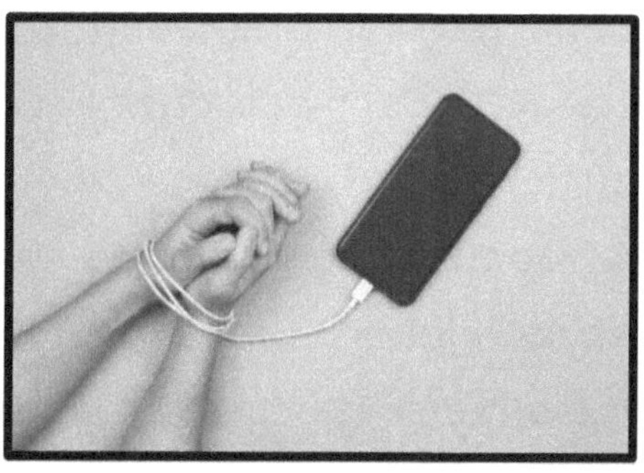

While cell phones have become an indispensable part of our modern lifestyle, offering various conveniences and advantages, it is essential to acknowledge that their pervasive use has brought about a concerning phenomenon recognized as phone addiction. This condition, often identified by certain researchers, involves individuals exhibiting symptoms that suggest a dependency on their devices, leading to detrimental impacts on their overall well-being.

The issue of phone addiction is particularly prominent among young adults, with research indicating that approximately 27.9% of individuals in this demographic group are considered addicted to their cell phones. This statistic sheds light on the prevalence of this modern-day challenge and underscores the importance of understanding its implications. It is crucial to recognize that excessive reliance on cell phones can result in a range of adverse effects, such as heightened levels of stress, disrupted sleep patterns, decreased productivity, and strained social relationships.

The constant urge to check notifications, scroll through social media feeds, or engage in excessive texting can significantly interfere with one's ability to focus on important tasks or fully engage in face-to-face interactions. This behavioral pattern, if left unaddressed, has the potential to erode the individual's mental and emotional well-being over time. It is evident that the allure of constant connectivity and instant gratification provided by cell phones has contributed to the rise of phone addiction, necessitating a balanced approach to technology usage and fostering healthy digital habits.

Cell phone addiction, also known as nomophobia, is a prevalent issue in today's society where individuals struggle to detach themselves from their mobile devices, leading to detrimental impacts on their daily lives and mental well-being. This addiction is characterized by an individual's compulsive need to constantly check their phone, even in situations where it is socially inappropriate or potentially harmful, demonstrating a strong reliance on the device for emotional comfort and social interaction.

The excessive use of cell phones can result in adverse consequences, affecting different aspects of a person's life including relationships, work productivity, and overall mental health. Individuals with cell phone addiction may neglect important responsibilities, experience increased stress and anxiety, and face difficulties in engaging in face-to-face interactions due to their constant digital presence. These behavioral patterns closely resemble those seen in traditional substance addictions, reinforcing the argument for recognizing cell phone addiction as a valid mental health concern.

Despite the clear parallels between cell phone addiction and established behavioral disorders like gambling addiction, it is worth noting that the official acknowledgment of cell phone addiction as a standalone diagnosis is notably absent from the DSM-5. This absence may be due to ongoing debates within the mental health community regarding the classification and criteria for behavioral addictions, underscoring the complexity of addressing emerging behavioral issues in a rapidly evolving technological landscape. However, the detrimental effects of cell phone addiction on individuals' lives emphasize the urgent need for further research and clinical consideration to better understand and address this modern-day challenge.

While cell phone addiction may not yet be officially recognized as a mental health disorder, its impact on individuals' lives is undeniable and warrants attention from both researchers and healthcare professionals. By exploring the underlying mechanisms of cell phone addiction and developing effective intervention strategies, we can work towards mitigating the harmful effects of excessive phone use and promoting healthier digital habits in today's interconnected world.

Smartphones have become ingrained in our daily lives due to a multitude of factors contributing to their addictive nature. When we delve into the reasons behind why smartphones are so difficult to pry from our grasp, we uncover a web of intricacies that captivate and consume our attention. It's not just the allure of the vibrant screens or the sleek designs; rather, it's the way in which these devices have been meticulously engineered to ensnare us, making it nearly impossible to resist their digital charms.

The warning of smartphones lies in their ability to provide us with instant gratification at every turn. The cacophony of sounds and vibrations emanating from our devices acts as a siren call, beckoning us to check for new messages, social media updates, or the latest notifications. With each buzz, ding, or ping, we find ourselves drawn deeper into the digital realm that these handheld marvels offer, unable to resist the allure of what might await us on the other side of that notification.

The array of entertainment options available at our fingertips further cements smartphones as an integral part of our daily routines. Whether it's the immersive gameplay of mobile apps, the endless scroll of social media feeds, or the personalized content tailored to our preferences, smartphones serve as a gateway to a world of endless diversion and engagement. The clever use of persuasive design tactics, such as infinite scrolling and push notifications, serves to keep us perpetually hooked, ensuring that we remain plugged in and connected to the digital whirlwind that surrounds us.

Smartphones have evolved beyond mere communication tools; they have become extensions of our very beings, seamlessly weaving themselves into the fabric of our existence. The addictive nature of these devices stems not only from their sleek designs and advanced technology but also from the psychological mechanisms at play, compelling us to constantly seek out the next hit of digital dopamine. As we navigate this landscape of constant connectivity and instant gratification, it becomes increasingly clear why smartphones are so challenging to set aside—they have become an indispensable part of our modern lives, blurring the lines between reality and the digital realm.

Nomophobia, which stands for the fear tied to being separated from one's mobile phone, is a modern-day anxiety that has become increasingly prevalent in today's technology-dependent society. This phobia manifests as a deep-rooted fear of missing out on important calls, messages, or notifications, leading individuals to feel a sense of unease or discomfort when their phone is not within reach. People experiencing nomophobia may exhibit symptoms such as restlessness, constant checking of their phone, and heightened anxiety levels.

Similarly, Textaphrenia, another phone-related fear, revolves around the distressing thought of being unable to send or receive text messages. This fear is characterized by a compulsive need to constantly check one's phone for new messages, and the fear of missing out on important or timely information. People suffering from Textaphrenia may feel a sense of isolation or disconnect when they are unable to engage in text-based communication, which can further exacerbate their anxiety levels.

On the other hand, Ringxiety, or phantom notification syndrome, describes the sensation of erroneously believing that a notification has been received on one's phone when in reality, there is no actual alert. This phenomenon can cause individuals to repeatedly check their phone in anticipation of a message or call, even when no such communication is forthcoming. Ringxiety can lead to feelings of frustration, heightened stress levels, and a sense of over-dependence on digital devices for communication.

Textiety, a related fear, is the anxious feeling associated with the need to respond to text messages immediately upon receiving them. People experiencing Textiety may feel overwhelmed by the constant influx of messages, leading to a sense of pressure to respond promptly. This fear of delayed responses or missing important information through text messages can contribute to heightened stress levels and a sense of being constantly on edge.

These modern-day phobias and anxieties surrounding mobile phones and text messaging highlight the significant impact of technology on our psychological well-being and social interactions. As society becomes increasingly reliant on digital communication, it is essential to be mindful of the potential mental health implications and seek ways to maintain a healthy balance between technology use and mental well-being.

You have developed a habit of incessantly reaching for your phone throughout the day, almost as though it has become an extension of your hand. This constant companionship with your device consumes a significant portion of your waking hours, filling them with endless scrolling and browsing. Even during the night, your compulsion lingers, prompting you to stir from sleep just to gaze at the screen, seeking solace in the glow of notifications that momentarily alleviate any feelings of disconnection.

However, the absence of your phone swiftly brings about a whirlwind of negative emotions that cloud your thoughts and sow discomfort within you. Anger, sadness, and anxiety converge upon you, casting a shadow of unease whenever you find yourself separated from your digital lifeline. It's as though a vital piece of yourself is missing, leaving you adrift in a sea of turbulent emotions that only recede once your phone is back in your grasp.

Yet, this reliance on your device has not been without consequence. The very act of engaging with your phone has led to incidents that transcend mere inconvenience. Perhaps it was a near-miss accident while texting and driving, a stark reminder of the danger inherent in divided attention. This wake-up call serves as a sobering reminder of the potential hazards that your phone usage can pose to yourself and others.

The pervasive nature of your phone usage has encroached upon your professional and personal spheres, blurring the boundaries between digital existence and real-life interactions. The time that should be dedicated to work or cultivating relationships is instead devoted to virtual engagements, jeopardizing the quality of your engagements and the depth of your connections.

Despite your earnest attempts to curb your phone usage, your efforts often prove short-lived, with temptation lurking around every corner. The siren call of notifications and updates proves too strong to resist, leading to a cycle of restriction and relapse that perpetuates the grip your phone has on you. Breaking free from this cycle of dependency and reclaiming control over your phone habits appears to be a daunting task, but one that is essential for regaining agency over your time and emotional well-being.

One way to identify if you are developing a phone addiction is through the observations of those around you. Often, it can be challenging to recognize this addiction in ourselves, but when someone close to you voices their concern about your phone usage patterns, it becomes a clear indicator that a problem may be arising. This concern typically manifests when they notice the excessive time you spend on your device, perhaps highlighting moments when you are engrossed in your phone rather than engaging with your surroundings. Their observations may extend to pointing out behaviors that suggest a dependency on your phone, such as constantly checking for notifications or being preoccupied with screen time even in social settings. These comments from others serve as an external perspective that mirrors your growing reliance on your phone and can be seen as a warning sign to take a step back and reassess your relationship with technology. By paying attention to these signals and reflecting on your phone habits in response to the feedback you receive, you can gain valuable insights into whether your phone usage has escalated to the point of addiction, prompting necessary adjustments to achieve a healthier balance in your daily life.

***

Who Is at Risk of Phone Addiction

Child to Elder Person

The exact number of individuals grappling with cell phone addiction remains elusive within the realm of research. This lack of precise quantification stems from the inherent difficulty in measuring such dependency accurately, as many studies rely on self-reported data, which is known to have limitations in its reliability and validity.

While susceptibility to cellphone addiction transcends age demographics, it predominantly manifests among the younger population, especially adolescents. Various studies suggest that approximately 20% to 30% of teenagers and young adults exhibit signs of phone addiction. Notably, adolescents exhibit a penchant for frequent phone usage, with this behavior gradually tapering off as individuals mature.

The age at which individuals acquire their first cell phone plays a pivotal role in their likelihood of developing addictive behaviors. Research indicates that those who gain access to phones at a young age are at a higher risk of exhibiting addictive tendencies compared to individuals who acquire phones later in life.

Understanding the nuanced interplay between age demographics, usage patterns, and addiction tendencies in relation to cell phones can shed light on the multifaceted nature of this prevalent modern-day issue.

Cell Phone Risk Between the Sexes

Both young boys and girls are at a higher risk of developing an addiction to their cell phones due to the prevalent use of smartphones in today's digital age. The accessibility and functionality of these devices have made them not just tools for communication but also sources of entertainment and connection. Moreover, the nature of phone usage differs slightly between genders, with girls often utilizing their devices primarily for social interaction. This trend can be attributed to the importance of social relationships and communication among adolescent girls, for whom peer connections play a crucial role in identity formation and emotional well-being.

On the other hand, boys tend to engage with their phones for similar social reasons but also show a notable affinity towards gaming applications. The integration of gaming features on smartphones has captured the interest of many young males, offering them a platform for entertainment and skill development. The engaging nature of mobile games, often designed with competitive and rewarding elements, can contribute to prolonged and intensive phone usage among boys.

The research indicates that males exhibit a higher inclination to use their phones in risky situations. This behavior may stem from a combination of factors, including impulsivity, sensation-seeking tendencies, and the desire for novel and stimulating experiences. The allure of taking risks while using a mobile device can lead to potentially harmful or dangerous behaviors, such as texting while driving or using the phone in unsafe environments.

In essence, understanding the distinct patterns of phone use among young boys and girls is crucial in addressing the issue of smartphone addiction and promoting healthy digital habits. By acknowledging the varying motivations and behaviors associated with phone usage, interventions and preventive strategies can be tailored to suit the specific needs and preferences of different gender groups, fostering responsible and balanced technology use among adolescents.

***

Sleeping issues of Smartphone addiction

Mobile use at bedtime (after the lights have been turned off), can cause poor sleep quality (PSQ) by various mechanisms. Due to the technology revolution, which has brought about a significant increase in mobile phone users owning smartphones, individuals now have the capability to access a wide range of activities on their devices. With smartphones granting access to the internet, social networks, video content, online chatting platforms, and gaming applications, users are exposed to highly stimulating material that can lead to detrimental effects on their sleep. This overexposure to engaging content, coupled with excessive mobile phone usage and the development of phone addiction, all contribute to a state of hyperarousal in the period leading up to bedtime. This hyperarousal, in turn, disrupts the natural transition to sleep, resulting in an overall decline in sleep quality.

The constant availability of these activities on smartphones means that individuals are more prone to engaging with their devices late into the night, further exacerbating the issue of poor sleep quality. In today's digital age, the convenience and allure of smartphones have made it increasingly challenging for users to disconnect from their devices, even when it interferes with their ability to achieve restful sleep. The pervasive nature of smartphone use at bedtime has led to a normalization of this behavior, with many individuals underestimating the impact it can have on their sleep patterns and overall well-being.

The addictive nature of smartphones and the instant gratification they provide through various forms of entertainment can create a cycle of dependency that reinforces the habit of using mobile devices right before bedtime. This dependency not only strengthens the association between smartphone use and bedtime but also diminishes the likelihood of adopting healthier bedtime routines that prioritize relaxation and preparation for sleep. As a result, the negative repercussions of mobile phone overuse on sleep quality continue to compound, leading to a detrimental cycle of poor sleep hygiene and suboptimal rest.

Restricting mobile phone use close to bedtime has been found, through research studies conducted in the field of sleep disturbances, to have tangible and positive effects on various aspects of sleep and cognitive functions. In a fascinating discovery, it was observed that reducing mobile phone use before sleep can significantly lower sleep latency - the time taken to fall asleep after getting into bed. This decrease in the time needed to transition into sleep not only enhances the overall quality of sleep but also reduces pre-sleep arousal levels, leading to a more relaxed and restful night's rest.

The benefits of limiting phone usage before bedtime extend beyond just promoting sound and restorative sleep. Individuals who adopted this simple change reported an increase in sleep duration, suggesting that minimizing exposure to screens and blue light has a direct impact on the body's natural circadian rhythm. This adjustment in behavior also positively influenced working memory, a crucial cognitive function essential for learning, problem-solving, and overall mental performance.

Given the prevalence and convenience of mobile phones in modern society, integrating such recommendations into daily routines can be a powerful tool in improving overall health and well-being. With mobile phones becoming an indispensable aspect of our lives over the past decade, it is increasingly important to be mindful of their potential impact on our sleep quality and cognitive abilities. By recognizing the effect of technology on our sleep health and incorporating practical changes, individuals can take proactive steps towards achieving a more balanced and fulfilling lifestyle.

In light of these compelling findings, experts in the field of sleep medicine and cognitive psychology advocate for a conscious effort to establish healthier bedtime routines that reduce reliance on electronic devices. Encouraging individuals to disconnect from their phones before sleep not only benefits their own wellness but also contributes to a broader societal shift towards prioritizing restful sleep and cognitive function. As we navigate the complex relationship between technology and health, this small adjustment in behavior presents a remarkable opportunity for individuals to reclaim control over their sleep patterns and mental acuity, leading to improved overall quality of life and productivity.

***

Social Media Addiction making many lives in danger

Social media addiction, a prevalent phenomenon in today's digitally connected world, often intertwines with phone addiction, forming a symbiotic relationship that can have profound effects on individuals' well-being. This coexistence has been repeatedly linked to various negative outcomes, such as reduced quality of sleep and heightened risks of depression, underscoring the detrimental impact that excessive screen time can have on both physical and mental health. Furthermore, studies have illuminated a concerning correlation between social media addiction and body perception issues, shedding light on how prolonged exposure to curated online content can distort one's self-image and lead to unrealistic beauty standards and self-comparisons.

The pervasive nature of social media platforms and the constant connectivity facilitated by smartphones have fostered an environment where individuals may find themselves increasingly dependent on these digital tools, sometimes to the detriment of their overall health and well-being. Moreover, the perceived need to constantly stay plugged in, fueled by the fear of missing out or the pressure to maintain a certain online presence, can exacerbate the addictive tendencies associated with social media and phone usage.

As individuals navigate the intricate web of social media interactions and digital communication, it is important to recognize the potential pitfalls of excessive engagement and to prioritize self-awareness and moderation in consumption. By fostering a balanced approach to technology usage and being mindful of the impact that social media and phone addiction can have, individuals can take proactive steps towards safeguarding their mental and physical health in an increasingly interconnected digital landscape.

***

Effects of Phone Addiction

Several research studies have highlighted the detrimental effects of excessive cell phone usage on human health, especially among the younger population. One area of concern is the impact on mental health, with prolonged screen time linked to increased feelings of depression, anxiety, and stress. Additionally, psychological well-being can be significantly compromised as individuals become more reliant on their smartphones for social interactions, leading to decreased face-to-face communication and potentially contributing to feelings of isolation and loneliness.

On the physical health front, the consequences of smartphone addiction are equally concerning. Extended periods of scrolling, typing, and staring at screens can result in various musculoskeletal issues, such as neck and back pain, as well as eye strain. Furthermore, excessive cell phone use before bedtime has been linked to disrupted sleep patterns, affecting both the quantity and quality of rest individuals get each night.

The negative impacts of cell phone overuse span across different aspects of well-being, highlighting the importance of setting boundaries and practicing moderation when it comes to technology usage. By recognizing these potential health risks and actively taking steps to limit screen time, individuals can promote better overall health and ensure a more balanced relationship with their devices.

Phone addiction can lead to a variety of mental health challenges and physical symptoms. Some of these include depression, anxiety, obsessive-compulsive disorder (OCD), attention deficit hyperactivity disorder (ADHD), alcohol use disorder, difficulties in cognitive-emotion regulation, impulsivity, impaired cognitive function, addiction to social networking, shyness, and low self-esteem.

The effects of phone addiction can manifest in physical discomforts such as muscle pain and stiffness, fatigue, blurry vision, dry eyes, red or irritated eyes, auditory illusions (mistakenly hearing your phone ring or vibrate when it's not), thumb or wrist pain. It can also result in loss of interest in activities you once enjoyed, insomnia and sleep disturbances, worsened school or work performance, heightened conflicts with your social group or family, feelings of irritability or unease in the absence of your phone, an increased risk of developing depression or anxiety, and putting yourself in dangerous situations by using your phone inappropriately.

The emotional toll of phone addiction can lead to feelings of guilt, helplessness, or loneliness when separated from your phone. The cumulative impact of these various consequences emphasizes the importance of recognizing and managing phone addiction to maintain overall well-being.

Cell phone addiction, a prevalent modern phenomenon, shares parallels with other forms of addiction due to its influence on dopamine, a critical neurotransmitter responsible for regulating pleasure sensations in the brain. When individuals engage in excessive cell phone use, research indicates a notable increase in the activation of dopamine-producing pathways, leading to heightened levels of this neurotransmitter being released. This surge in dopamine release contributes significantly to the reinforcement of technology use behaviors, creating a cycle wherein the allure of cell phone interaction becomes increasingly compelling over time.

As users repeatedly engage with their cell phones, the escalating dopamine response reinforces this behavior, essentially conditioning individuals to seek out these devices with greater frequency. Consequently, the pleasurable feelings associated with heightened dopamine levels can serve as a driving force behind the insatiable urge to utilize cell phones continuously. This profound connection between dopamine release and cell phone usage underscores the neurobiological underpinnings of addiction, shedding light on the intricate mechanisms through which technology can exert a profound hold over individuals.

The pervasive nature of cell phone addiction extends beyond mere dopamine manipulation, encompassing various psychological and behavioral facets. Notably, individuals struggling with excessive cell phone use may experience a range of emotional responses, including anxiety, stress, and agitation when separated from their devices. This emotional dependence on cell phones further reinforces the addictive cycle, as individuals seek solace and distraction through constant connectivity, perpetuating the cycle of dependence and withdrawal.

In essence, the intricate interplay between dopamine regulation, psychological dependence, and behavioral reinforcement elucidates the complex nature of cell phone addiction. By delving into the multifaceted mechanisms through which cell phones impact brain chemistry and behavior, we gain a deeper understanding of the pervasive allure and challenges associated with overcoming this contemporary form of addiction.

***

How to break this Smrt phone Addiction

Breaking any type of addiction isn't easy, but it is possible with dedication, support, and the right strategies in place. When embarking on the journey to overcome an addiction, the first crucial step is to recognize and understand the impact it has on your life and relationships. By facing the reality of how addiction is affecting you, you set the foundation for change and growth.

Upon acknowledging the need to break free from the grips of addiction, there are several constructive steps you can take to facilitate your recovery. One essential aspect is to delve into the underlying reasons that fuel your addiction. For instance, research suggests that excessive phone usage might stem from a desire to escape or cope with personal challenges. By identifying the root causes of your addictive behavior, you empower yourself to confront these issues directly and implement healthier coping mechanisms.

Seeking professional help through therapy can be instrumental in navigating the complexities of addiction recovery. Therapeutic approaches like cognitive behavioral therapy (CBT) have demonstrated effectiveness in assisting individuals in overcoming various addictions by reshaping harmful thought patterns and behaviors. Additionally, therapies such as contingency management, motivational interviewing, and couples counseling can provide tailored support to address addiction-related challenges and strengthen interpersonal relationships affected by addictive behaviors.

While the path to recovery from addiction can be arduous, it is certainly achievable with self-awareness, therapeutic intervention, and a commitment to personal growth and well-being. By taking proactive steps and seeking appropriate support, individuals can pave the way towards a life free from the shackles of addiction.

Rediscover Paper

If you've ever noticed that reading a tangible book elicits a deeper sense of fulfillment compared to reading off a digital tablet, your observation is grounded in reality. The intrinsic appeal of physical books lies not only in their ability to shield us from myriad distractions prevalent in the digital realm but also in their propensity to enhance our focus and cognitive awareness. Shedding light on this phenomenon, a comprehensive review published in 2019 within the esteemed Journal of Research in Reading posited that our cognitive processes exhibit heightened levels of efficacy when we turn the pages of a printed book as opposed to scrolling through content on a screen.

The act of engrossing ourselves in a traditional book fosters a unique kinship between the reader and the text, forming an intimate bond that can sometimes be difficult to replicate in the digital domain. Enveloped within the pages of a physical book, our senses become attuned to the tactile sensation of flipping through paper, absorbing the distinct scent of ink, and relishing the comforting weight of the volume in our hands. These sensory experiences, intertwined with the literary content, create a holistic reading experience that transcends mere information consumption and ventures into the realm of profound intellectual engagement.

Moreover, the palpable nature of printed books provides a sense of permanence and authenticity that is often absent in the transient world of digital information. The act of physically turning pages and visually tracking progress through a book imbues the reading process with a tangible rhythm, guiding our comprehension and retention of the material with a sense of structured progression. In contrast, the fluid, dynamic nature of digital screens can sometimes lead to a disjointed reading experience characterized by fragmented attention and decreased comprehension.

In essence, the traditional medium of books embodies a timeless allure that resonates deeply with our cognitive processes and sensory perceptions. The intimate connection forged between reader and book during the tactile exploration of printed pages evokes a sense of intellectual immersion and concentration that are essential for absorbing complex ideas and narratives. As we navigate the evolving landscape of reading formats, it is essential to recognize the enduring value of physical books in cultivating a profound and enriching reading experience that transcends the superficial distractions of the digital age.

Limit Yourself to One Screen at a Time

In the modern age, where distractions are as abundant as opportunities, our ability to maintain focus and concentration becomes increasingly challenging. When we find ourselves endeavoring a task and succumb to the temptation of mindlessly scrolling through various screens, our brain's functionality becomes disrupted, sending signals that resemble a state of chaos. According to Fox, renowned for their expertise in cognitive studies, multitasking represents a detrimental practice to our mental processes. The mere act of shifting our attention from a primary task to indulge in a minor distraction, such as checking a message or clicking onto another window, initiates a chain reaction within our brains that can take precious minutes to realign back to the initial task at hand.

Habit-forming behaviors play a crucial role in combating this ongoing battle with divided attention. By consciously training ourselves to focus on one screen at a time, we not only enhance our concentration levels but also pave the way for potentially increased enjoyment in our daily activities. This emphasis on singular engagement with a particular task fosters a sense of mindfulness and attentiveness, qualities that are fundamental in navigating a world constantly vying for our attention.

In the realm of productivity and cognitive performance, the notion of multitasking is often falsely lauded as a desirable skill. However, the reality is far from this perception. Research has repeatedly demonstrated that attempting multiple tasks simultaneously leads to a decrease in efficiency and a spike in mental fatigue. Our brains are not designed to effortlessly switch between tasks, contrary to what popular belief may suggest. Thus, by consciously choosing to resist the allure of simultaneous activities on different screens, we are not only safeguarding our mental wellbeing but also promoting a culture of focused engagement that ultimately leads to greater personal fulfillment and achievement.

Protect Your Body

According to the American Academy of Child & Adolescent Psychiatry, teenagers spend an average of nine hours daily engaging with devices featuring digital screens. This extensive screen time exposes them to the risk of digital eye strain, a common issue that manifests through symptoms like eye dryness, blurred vision, and headaches, as highlighted in a 2016 report published in Optometry in Practice.

To alleviate the strain on your eyes caused by prolonged screen exposure, experts recommend adhering to the 20-20-20 rule, which entails taking a break every 20 minutes to focus on an object located 20 feet away for about 20 seconds. Furthermore, it is essential to remember the importance of blinking frequently to keep your eyes moist and reduce the likelihood of experiencing discomfort.

Beyond eye-related concerns, studies have shown that excessive texting can contribute to physical ailments such as "text neck" and "smartphone thumb," as documented in a comprehensive 2019 study featured in the Journal of Public Health. To mitigate the adverse effects of prolonged texting, it is advisable to adjust the positioning of your device to eye level to prevent excessive bending of the neck. Additionally, adopting a variety of typing techniques that involve different fingers can help alleviate strain on the thumb and reduce the risk of inflammation, irritation, and pain associated with repetitive texting motions.

Remember, it is crucial to intersperse screen usage with regular breaks to prevent the onset of these issues and maintain overall eye and physical health. By practicing these recommended strategies, you can ensure that your screen time remains productive and comfortable, promoting your overall well-being in the digital age.

***

Some tips to overcome phone addiction on their own

While addictions often require professional help, not all people will want to go that route. If you want to try to get over phone addiction on your own, there are several practical strategies you can implement to help curb your cellphone usage.

One effective method is to invest in a cellphone lockbox that operates on a timer, allowing the box to open only after a specific amount of time has passed. This physical barrier can serve as a deterrent, limiting your access to your phone and discouraging impulsive usage.

Another step you can take is to assess the apps on your phone and remove those that consume the majority of your time. By decluttering your device and focusing on essential applications, you can streamline your usage and reduce the temptation to constantly check your phone.

Disabling notifications on your phone can be highly beneficial. This simple adjustment eliminates the constant distractions caused by notifications, helping you break the habit of reflexively reaching for your phone every time it buzzes or chimes.

To further distance yourself from your phone, consider charging it in an inaccessible location. Placing your phone out of arm's reach while it charges can create a physical barrier that encourages you to detach from its constant presence.

Engaging in alternative activities that you enjoy can also redirect your attention away from your phone. Whether it's reading a book, going for a walk, or pursuing a hobby, finding fulfilling and engaging pastimes can help you reduce your reliance on your device.

If you're particularly committed to reducing your smartphone usage, you may even consider switching to a non-smartphone. Opting for a less technologically advanced device can significantly limit your access to distracting apps and features, promoting a healthier and more balanced relationship with technology.

While overcoming phone addiction can be challenging, taking proactive steps such as utilizing a cellphone lockbox, removing time-consuming apps, disabling notifications, charging your phone out of reach, exploring alternative activities, and potentially switching to a non-smartphone can all contribute to breaking the cycle of excessive phone usage and regaining control over your screen time.

***

Prevent Smartphone Addiction

The most effective strategy to combat phone addiction is through practicing avoidance. By consciously using your phone only when it is truly necessary, you can steer clear of falling into the trap of addictive behaviors associated with excessive screen time. This entails taking a proactive approach in managing your phone usage by removing any non-essential apps that may serve as potential catalysts for addiction. Instead of getting lost in mindless scrolling, redirect your focus towards meaningful interactions and quality time spent with loved ones in alternative ways.

For parents navigating the challenge of controlling their young children's access to phones, establishing clear boundaries is key. Setting specific guidelines for phone usage and permitting its use only under monitored conditions can help curb the likelihood of addiction taking root. Another preventive measure is delaying the introduction of smartphones until a certain age, especially during the crucial teenage years when susceptibility to addiction is highest. This deliberate delay in granting phone privileges can create a safeguard against premature exposure to potential risks associated with excessive screen time.

In instances where a child's safety necessitates the provision of a phone, opting for a device that restricts app downloads is a prudent choice. By selecting a phone that limits access to potentially addictive apps, you can strike a balance between connectivity and responsible usage. This ensures that your child remains connected for essential communication purposes while mitigating the risks of falling prey to time-consuming applications that fuel addictive behaviors. Ultimately, by adopting these preventive measures and mindful approaches to phone usage, you can cultivate healthy habits and promote a balanced relationship with technology among children and adolescents.

***

Health problems of Smart phone addiction

It is quite common for individuals to experience anxiety when they go for a few hours without checking their phones. This fear stems from the concern that by not checking, they might miss out on something important. A prevalent effect of this behavior is that people develop a strong attachment to their phones, to the extent where they feel uneasy leaving the house without them or even turning off notifications. As a result, there develops an incessant need to constantly stay connected and be updated throughout the day, leading to what is commonly known as FOMO, or the fear of missing out.

This fear of missing out often manifests as a persistent urge to check social media platforms, even when there may not be any new content. People tend to continuously browse through their online feeds, rather than waiting for notifications, in order to remain updated on what others are doing. This behavior can evoke feelings of inadequacy or loneliness, as individuals compare their own lives to the seemingly busy and exciting activities portrayed by others on social media. The constant exposure to such curated and often exaggerated content can create a distorted sense of reality, making one feel as though they are not as popular or socially active as their online peers.

Due to the prevalent use of smartphones among women, there has been a noticeable increase in health issues such as thyroid problems, a rapid decline in eye health leading to the early need for glasses, and a rise in various mental health concerns. Additionally, the excessive use of smartphones has been linked to disruptions in menstrual cycles and other related issues affecting women's reproductive health. The constant exposure to screens and blue light emitted by smartphones can contribute to hormonal imbalances, which in turn may lead to a variety of health complications impacting women. Moreover, the sedentary lifestyle often associated with smartphone usage can exacerbate these health issues, further emphasizing the importance of maintaining a balanced approach to technology use. As women continue to rely heavily on smartphones for communication, work, and entertainment, it is crucial for individuals to be mindful of potential health risks and to prioritize self-care practices that promote overall well-being. By acknowledging the impact of smartphone usage on women's health and taking proactive steps to mitigate associated risks, individuals can strive to achieve a healthier and more balanced lifestyle in the digital age.

The modern age of technology and social media has significantly impacted how individuals perceive their own lives in comparison to others'. The pressure to constantly stay connected and updated through smartphones has given rise to a pervasive fear of being left out or not measuring up to the seemingly glamorous lifestyles showcased online. This phenomenon highlights the importance of striking a balance between digital connectivity and personal well-being, as excessive reliance on technology can often lead to feelings of isolation and inadequacy.

Another detrimental effect stemming from mobile addiction is the emergence of various health issues among users. The excessive use of mobile devices often leads individuals to confine themselves indoors, depriving them of regular physical activity that is essential for maintaining good health. By being engrossed in their phones, people forego engaging in outdoor activities that could otherwise provide a healthier alternative to screen time. Furthermore, the habit of keeping phones under pillows, especially while sleeping, poses risks to one's well-being. The constant urge to check for updates even during the night disrupts sleep patterns, causing individuals to wake up intermittently and resulting in fatigue during the day. Consequently, this disruption in sleep impacts one's ability to function optimally, particularly in environments like school where concentration and alertness are crucial. The pervasive nature of mobile addiction further exacerbates these health concerns by keeping individuals perpetually tethered to their devices, impeding their ability to disconnect and rest adequately. Ultimately, the prevalence of mobile addiction manifests not only in mental and emotional repercussions but also in physiological consequences that can significantly impact overall well-being.

Relationship Issues:

Relationship issues stemming from mobile addiction can have a profound impact on couples as they increasingly prioritize their phones over quality time with their partners. This shift in attention can lead to feelings of neglect and isolation, creating a sense of disconnect within the relationship. As individuals become more engrossed in their digital devices, the emotional bond between them weakens, and they may find themselves yearning for the intimacy that has been replaced by scrolling through endless feeds and notifications.

The rise of social media exacerbates these relationship challenges by presenting an unrealistic depiction of others' lives, fueling envy and insecurity. Couples may compare their own mundane routines to the seemingly glamorous lifestyles portrayed online, leading to a perception of inadequacy and disappointment in their own circumstances. The constant exposure to curated representations of happiness and success can breed discontentment and strain the foundation of even the most steadfast relationships.

The erosion of communication caused by mobile addiction can give rise to misunderstandings and conflict in relationships. When individuals prioritize virtual interactions over meaningful conversations with their partners, essential emotional connections are neglected, leading to a breakdown in trust and mutual understanding. This breakdown can manifest in jealousy, resentment, and a deep-seated sense of dissatisfaction within the relationship.

In essence, by succumbing to the allures of mobile addiction and social media consumption, couples risk sacrificing the authentic connections that are vital for a healthy and fulfilling relationship. It becomes imperative for individuals to recognize the detrimental effects of excessive screen time on their relationships and prioritize real-world interactions that nurture emotional intimacy and understanding. Only through conscious efforts to limit digital distractions and invest in meaningful moments together can couples safeguard the strength and resilience of their bond amidst the pervasive influence of technology.

Stress And Anxiety:

Stress and anxiety often manifest as significant repercussions of mobile addiction, primarily due to the inherent need for individuals to constantly engage with their devices, causing them to feel overwhelmed by the fear of missing out on potentially engaging activities. This compulsion to incessantly check for updates can lead to heightened stress levels, as individuals may worry about missing out on opportunities or exciting events elsewhere. The pervasive nature of this behavior creates a persistent sensation that everyone else is participating in more stimulating activities, exacerbating the stress and anxiety associated with feeling disconnected or left out.

The reliance on mobile devices for notifications and updates can have detrimental effects on mental well-being. When individuals fail to receive or notice a notification, it can trigger a cycle of compulsive behavior, such as repeatedly refreshing online platforms in search of new information. This behavior not only contributes to increased stress but also hampers the ability to fully engage in other activities or spend quality time with loved ones. The constant need for digital stimulation can impede individuals from being present in the moment, distracting them from the surroundings and experiences during daily routines or leisure activities.

The pervasive nature of mobile addiction perpetuates a cycle of stress and anxiety by fostering feelings of inadequacy, fear of missing out, and the constant need for digital validation. This continuous cycle of checking for updates and notifications can lead to heightened levels of stress, impacting individuals' ability to focus on meaningful interactions and activities beyond the confines of their devices.

Impact On Society And Family Life:

The influence of technology on society has resulted in a notable increase in distraction among individuals. Consequently, many struggle to focus on singular tasks without their thoughts wandering elsewhere. This trend poses potential challenges, particularly in academic or professional settings, where concentration is paramount. When individuals are unable to immediately immerse themselves in their work or studies, the quality of their output may suffer, hindering their overall productivity.

The pervasive nature of technology has impacted personal connections and communication patterns, with people tending to prioritize online interactions over face-to-face conversations. The constant accessibility to social media platforms like Facebook and Twitter often leads to a sense of missing out on significant updates and events, perpetuating the fear of being left behind. This can further exacerbate feelings of anxiety and dissatisfaction, fuelled by the comparison to curated online personas.

In the context of familial relationships, the reliance on technology for social connection has caused a reduction in meaningful interactions between family members. Rather than engaging in heartfelt conversations and spending quality time together, individuals may find themselves preoccupied with digital distractions, such as scrolling through feeds or responding to messages. This shift in dynamics can contribute to a sense of disconnect within families, as genuine bonding experiences become overshadowed by virtual engagements.

Overall, the omnipresence of technology in modern society has fundamentally altered the way people engage with their surroundings, work, and personal relationships. Addressing the impact of these changes is crucial in promoting a balanced approach to technology usage and fostering meaningful connections in an increasingly digital world.

***

How to Maintain Good relationships with family

Avoid showing smartphones to kids during meals time and don't entertain them with showing mobile videos etc. It spoils their future and health. Encouraging healthy habits during meals can have a significant impact on children's overall well-being. When children are constantly exposed to smartphones and mobile videos during mealtimes, it not only distracts them from enjoying their food but also hinders their ability to develop social skills and proper eating habits. Children who are engaged in screen time during meals are more likely to experience obesity and other health issues later in life.

Exposing children to excessive screen time at a young age can have long-term negative effects on their cognitive development and mental health. By limiting their exposure to smartphones and mobile videos during meals, parents can create a more conducive environment for meaningful interactions and proper nourishment. It is important for children to learn the value of healthy eating habits and social engagement from an early age, as these practices can lay the foundation for their future well-being.

By avoiding the use of smartphones as a source of entertainment during meals, parents can help children develop better self-regulation skills and improve their attention span. Children who are constantly stimulated by screens may struggle with focusing on tasks and engaging in real-life interactions. Therefore, setting boundaries around screen time during meals can support children in building resilience and developing healthier lifestyles.

The impact of avoiding smartphones and mobile videos during meals extends beyond mere distractions; it plays a crucial role in shaping children's future health and well-being. By prioritizing quality time and healthy eating habits during meals, parents can set their children up for a brighter and more balanced future.

Don't allow mobile inside Bed rooms:

"Many individuals rely on their phones as alarm clocks," explained Greenfield. He cautioned against the common temptation of falling into social media distraction when reaching for the phone to turn off the alarm. For better sleep hygiene, it is advised that one keeps their phone out of the bedroom at night and opts for a traditional alarm clock instead.

Taitz, a renowned psychologist and author, pointed out that using your phone in bed may hinder intimacy with your partner. She recommended establishing the bed as a tech-free sanctuary to foster closer connections and enhance opportunities for both emotional bonding and physical intimacy. By eliminating screens from the bedroom, not only can one improve their relationship dynamics but also promote a more restful sleep environment.

The detrimental effects of screens at bedtime extend beyond relationship implications. The blue light emitted by devices can disrupt the body's natural sleep cycle by tricking the brain into perceiving it as daytime, hindering the ability to relax and fall asleep easily. Therefore, it is vital to prioritize screen-free habits before bedtime to ensure quality rest and overall well-being.

***

Common relationships to face Challenges

In today's digital age, it has become increasingly common for relationships to face challenges due to the influence of smartphones. The ease of maintaining secret relationships through mobile phone chats has created a breeding ground for distrust and suspicion. Many individuals find themselves drawn to the allure of these forbidden connections, leading to a disconnection in their primary relationships.

When we consider the relationship dynamics between husbands and wives, it often feels like going through the motions rather than truly experiencing life together. Routine arguments and constant doubts overshadow moments that should be filled with love and connection. The very foundation of trust is eroded, leaving both partners feeling isolated and disheartened.

To navigate this modern landscape, it is crucial for partners to communicate openly and authentically within the comfort of their own homes. By prioritizing quality time together and making a conscious effort to disconnect from the digital world, couples can safeguard the integrity of their relationships. Implementing a practice of switching off mobile devices upon returning home can create a conducive environment for meaningful interactions, fostering genuine connection and intimacy.

Ultimately, by recognizing the pitfalls of smartphone distractions and actively working towards strengthening the bond between partners, relationships can be preserved and nurtured in a way that promotes mutual respect and understanding. It is through these intentional actions that couples can reignite the spark that initially brought them together, paving the way for a fulfilling and harmonious partnership.

If it is a big family, consider gathering everyone together for meals to share not only food but also delightful conversations centered around various topics of interest. Opt for meaningful interactions over mindlessly scrolling through smartphones, which not only consumes time but can also lead to detrimental consequences on both mental and physical health. Prioritize fostering love and affection among family members as this is key to nurturing strong relationships and maintaining harmonious dynamics within the family unit. Dedicate quality time to engaging with children by taking part in outdoor activities, engaging in playtime, captivating them with intriguing stories, actively listening to their thoughts and whimsical musings, and overall immersing yourself in the joy of their innocence and exuberance. Embrace the beauty of nature and instill a deep appreciation for the natural world by cultivating a lifestyle that is rooted in its serenity and wonder. By following these practices, you can create a rich tapestry of shared experiences and lasting memories that will undoubtedly enrich your family life and create a foundation of happiness and togetherness for years to come.

Avoid purchasing a mobile device for every individual within the household, as this could potentially limit the physical space available for communal activities such as sitting together and engaging in conversation. It is important to consider that excessive screen time and isolation resulting from everyone having their own mobile device may contribute to a variety of mental health challenges that individuals could encounter. By promoting a shared environment without the distraction of individual devices, opportunities for meaningful interactions and social connections can be nurtured, fostering a sense of togetherness and emotional well-being within the home. Encouraging face-to-face communication and bonding moments among family members can help mitigate the negative impact of constant screen usage on mental health. Additionally, creating a balance between technology use and interpersonal relationships can lead to a more harmonious living environment, where individuals feel supported and connected to one another beyond the confines of digital screens. Prioritizing human connection over technology dependency is essential in promoting mental wellness and building strong, resilient family dynamics that prioritize authentic interaction and emotional support.

If you find that owning a mobile phone for making calls is an essential need, it might be preferable to opt for a traditional mobile phone rather than investing in a smartphone. This choice can help in minimizing distractions that come with smartphones, such as engaging in video watching, social media browsing, and other digital entertainment. It is crucial to remember that the usage of smartphones in front of children can significantly influence their behavior and attitudes towards technology. By being mindful of our own smartphone use in the presence of children, we can actively guide and influence them positively. Children tend to mimic the behaviors they observe, so demonstrating responsible and restricted smartphone usage can help prevent them from becoming overly reliant on or addicted to these devices. Striking a balance between utilizing technology for its benefits while also setting boundaries on its usage can empower children to develop a healthy relationship with smartphones and other digital tools. Ultimately, making conscious decisions about our smartphone habits and considering the impact it has on younger generations can contribute to fostering a more balanced and mindful approach to technology in our lives.

Encouraging children to delve into the remarkable healing powers of nature rather than remaining idle at home, engrossed in television screens and smartphone activities, stands as a pivotal aspect of their holistic development. It is incumbent upon adults to serve as exemplary role models by embracing these teachings themselves before imparting them upon the younger generation. Through immersive outdoor experiences and hands-on activities that foster an appreciation for the interconnectedness between nature and well-being, children can cultivate a deep-rooted respect for the environment and its inherent healing properties. By steering children away from sedentary lifestyles and towards dynamic engagement with the natural world, we empower them to forge a profound connection with their surroundings, thereby enriching their physical, mental, and emotional well-being. Embracing this ethos not only cultivates a sense of responsibility towards ecological sustainability but also nurtures a curiosity and reverence for the bountiful gifts that nature has to offer. Ultimately, by fostering a culture of environmental stewardship and mindfulness, we equip children with the tools to lead more enriched and fulfilling lives, in harmony with the natural world.

We must make a conscious effort to return to embracing a simpler way of life, one that doesn't solely rely on the constant presence of smartphones. Embracing the ritual of reading books is a wonderful habit that not only enhances knowledge but also cultivates a sense of tranquility. Let us encourage everyone around us to dedicate more time to immersing themselves in the world of literature and enjoying the calming melodies of soothing music to unwind and de-stress.

Furthermore, ensuring a good night's sleep at the proper time and consuming nutritious, hygienic meals are essential components in maintaining a healthy lifestyle. It is important to not become ensnared in the alluring yet consuming world of smartphones, which can often detract from the simple joys of life. Let's refocus our attention on the beauty of tangible experiences and meaningful interactions, connecting with others and the world around us without the constant distraction of technology.

By prioritizing activities that nourish our minds and bodies, such as reading, listening to music, maintaining a proper sleep schedule, and eating well, we can break free from the grip of our smartphones and rediscover the richness of a balanced and fulfilling life. Let us lead by example and inspire those around us to cultivate healthy habits that promote well-being and a deeper appreciation for the world we live in.

When to Contact a Healthcare Provider

If you find yourself in a situation where the excessive use of your phone is starting to dominate your daily routines and interactions, or if your close friends and family members have expressed concerns about your screen time habits, it might be a crucial moment to consider reaching out for professional support and guidance to regain control over your digital usage.

One effective step towards addressing this issue is to reach out to your primary healthcare provider for recommendations on qualified therapists or mental health professionals who specialize in managing technology addiction and related concerns. These professionals can offer you personalized guidance and therapeutic interventions to help you develop healthier digital habits and regain a sense of balance in your life.

Alternatively, you may also want to explore the possibility of engaging in a digital detox program. A digital detox involves taking a deliberate break from using electronic devices such as smartphones, tablets, and computers for a specified period. This intentional hiatus from technology allows you to disconnect from constant digital stimulation, reset your relationship with screens, and recalibrate your focus towards more meaningful offline activities and interactions.

By seeking professional help or committing to a digital detox, you are taking proactive steps towards addressing the challenges associated with excessive phone usage and reclaiming agency over your screen time habits. Remember, it's essential to prioritize your well-being and mental health by actively seeking support and exploring strategies that can help you strike a healthier balance between technology use and real-world experiences.

While problematic cell phone use is not officially recognized in the DSM-5, it exhibits significant parallels with traditional behavioral addictions. Individuals grappling with a phone addiction often struggle to disengage from their devices, leading to a diminished interest in previously enjoyable activities due to excessive screen time. This phenomenon predominantly affects adolescents and young adults, placing them at a higher susceptibility to developing such dependencies.

Manifestations of phone addiction encompass a range of symptoms, including heightened irritability or negative emotions when separated from one's phone, an inability to sustain prolonged periods without phone access, and the harmful impact of excessive phone usage on both physical and mental well-being.

Despite the detrimental ramifications associated with phone addiction, various strategies can be employed to combat this issue effectively. One avenue involves seeking professional assistance from a therapist equipped to address addictive behavior patterns, while alternative approaches involve implementing self-regulatory techniques geared towards managing and reducing phone usage habits. By proactively addressing phone addiction through these proactive measures, individuals can reclaim control over their phone usage habits and restore balance to their lives.

***

Inspiring Real story of a village

A village in Maharashtra's Sangli district, situated amidst the bustling chaos of electronic gadgets and social media platforms in modern life, has taken a remarkable step to lead its residents towards a "digital detox" every evening.

The transformation initiates with a melodious siren echoing from a local temple precisely at 7 pm, serving as a gentle reminder for individuals to bid adieu to their mobile phones, gadgets, and televised distractions. As the evening unfolds, the silence of digital absence creates an atmosphere conducive to cultivating the virtues of reading, studying, and engaging in heart-to-heart conversations. The tranquility reigns until 8.30 pm, marked by the melodious chime of a second alarm signifying the end of the detox period.

The visionary behind this innovative concept is none other than Vijay Mohite, the devoted sarpanch of Mohityanche Vadgaon village. The enthusiastic participation of the residents breathes life into this novel exercise, setting a precedent for a community-driven approach towards reclaiming invaluable time lost to the digital deluge.

In a conversation with PTI, Sarpanch Mohite sheds light on the scourge of prolonged screen time exacerbated by the exigencies of the COVID-19 lockdown. The influx of virtual classes tethered young minds to screens long after the school day, while parents found solace in extended TV viewing hours. The consequences were stark — a generation growing lethargic, alienated from the joys of reading and writing, ensnared by the digital labyrinth.

Witnessing the detrimental impact firsthand, Mohite envisioned a solution rooted in simplicity — a respite from the digital din. The distinguishing hours between 7 pm and 8.30 pm now stand as a sanctuary free from the grip of screens. Mobile phones are set aside, televisions are powered down, paving the way for a revival of traditional pursuits like reading, studying, writing, and heartfelt dialogues. To ensure adherence to this regimen, a dedicated committee oversees the implementation across different wards of the village.

Focusing on the dire necessity of this shift, a proactive student, Gayatri Nikam, echoes the sentiment of lost potential amidst peers entrapped by the allure of screens. Amidst power outages and daily distractions, she underscores the crucial need for structured study time, indifferent to the whims of technology.

Anecdotal evidence from the village unveils a household narrative dominated by the drone of television serials, instead of the delightful hum of shared activities. The absence of parental oversight leaves the youth adrift in the digital ocean, bereft of the anchor of discipline.

With the novel digital detox in place, a heartening transformation unfolds within the village's confines. Children immerse themselves in the realm of study, parents rediscover the joy of literary pursuits, and households resonate with the harmonious symphony of productive endeavors. No longer a tale of scattered attention and missed opportunities, these evenings bear witness to a shared commitment towards growth and enrichment.

Drawing inspiration from a broader canvas, recent reports emerge of the Jain community in Raisen, Madhya Pradesh observing a "digital fast," marking a 24-hour respite from the virtual world during the paryushan parva. Through these unified efforts, the fabric of society evolves, weaving threads of conscious disconnection from the digital cacophony, reminiscent of a bygone era of simplicity and harmony.

***

Story of Mumbai Villages

MUMBAI (Thomson Reuters Foundation) - Several villages in the western Indian state of Gujarat have recently implemented restrictions prohibiting girls and single women from possessing mobile phones, asserting that such devices serve as a distraction from their academic pursuits. The directive, which has been initiated in a few villages across the Mehsana and Banaskantha districts in Gujarat, has been gaining momentum with additional villages joining the movement, as confirmed by Ranjit Singh Thakor, the president of the Mehsana district council.

According to Thakor, the prohibition targets girls under 18 years of age and unmarried women, aiming to ensure that the absence of mobile phones aids in maintaining their focus on education and prevents them from potentially encountering adverse situations. He stated in a telephone conversation with the Thomson Reuters Foundation that the intent behind the ban is to enable the young women to concentrate on their studies without the influence of technological distractions. Thakor further emphasized that girls should pursue education, transition into marriage, and subsequently consider obtaining mobile phones, with the provision that they may utilize their fathers' phones at home if necessary during this interim period.

This initiative is not the first instance in which Indian villages have introduced such regulations. In past years, several villages in the eastern state of Bihar had similarly imposed bans on mobile phone ownership among young women, citing concerns that the devices were impinging upon the societal fabric by potentially facilitating elopements. The move sparked contention among activists who denounced it as an infringement on personal freedoms and highlighted the risks posed to women's safety by depriving them of access to means of communication and protection.

India stands as the world's second-largest market for mobile phones, boasting a user base exceeding 1 billion individuals. The ban enforced in Gujarat's villages emerges against the backdrop of Prime Minister Narendra Modi's advocacy for the Digital India initiative, which endeavors to bridge the digital divide by extending high-speed Internet connectivity to rural areas. Thakor disclosed that individuals contravening the ban in Mehsana district would be subject to fines amounting to approximately 2,100 rupees ($31), while those providing information leading to enforcement would receive rewards. Furthermore, he specified that female university students are exempt from the prohibition, recognizing the necessity of mobile phones for their academic pursuits.

This measure has garnered support primarily within the Thakor caste across the state, reflecting a collective effort to uphold the initiative. Nonetheless, Gaurav Dahiya, the district development officer for Banaskantha district, revealed that while some villages have an informal regulation stipulating the ban for girls' safety, compliance appears limited. The informal rule, established by village elders, underscores the purported motive of safeguarding girls from potential risks posed by mobile phone usage, yet its efficacy remains questionable due to low adherence rates.

Research illustrates the transformative impact of mobile phone ownership on the lives of individuals residing in rural areas, particularly in regions with inadequate connectivity. A study conducted in Tanzania, for instance, underscored the substantial positive effects of mobile phones on women's businesses and overall livelihoods. However, in both Tanzania and India, a prevailing trend persists wherein male members often exercise control over phone ownership, especially in rural households where a single device may be shared among family members.

***